this coloring books belongs to

....

test your color

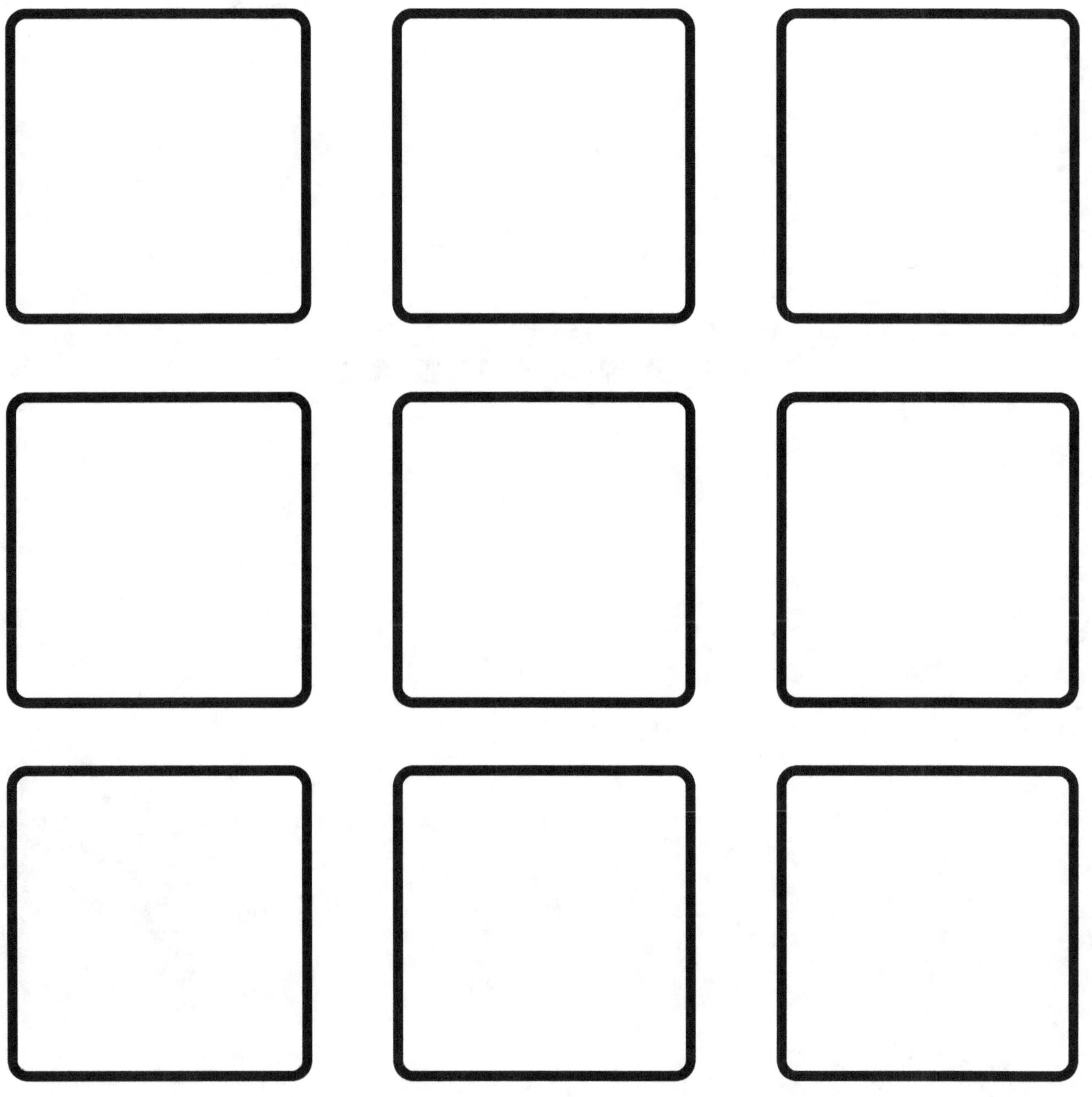

thank you,

..love you

thank you,

..love you

thank you,

..love you

thank you,

..love you

thank you,

..love you

thank you,

..love you

thank you,

..love you

thank you,

..love you

thank you,

..love you

thank you,

..love you

thank you,

..love you

thank you,

..love you

thank you,

..love you

thank you,

..love you

thank you,

..love you

thank you,

..love you

thank you,

..love you

thank you,

..love you

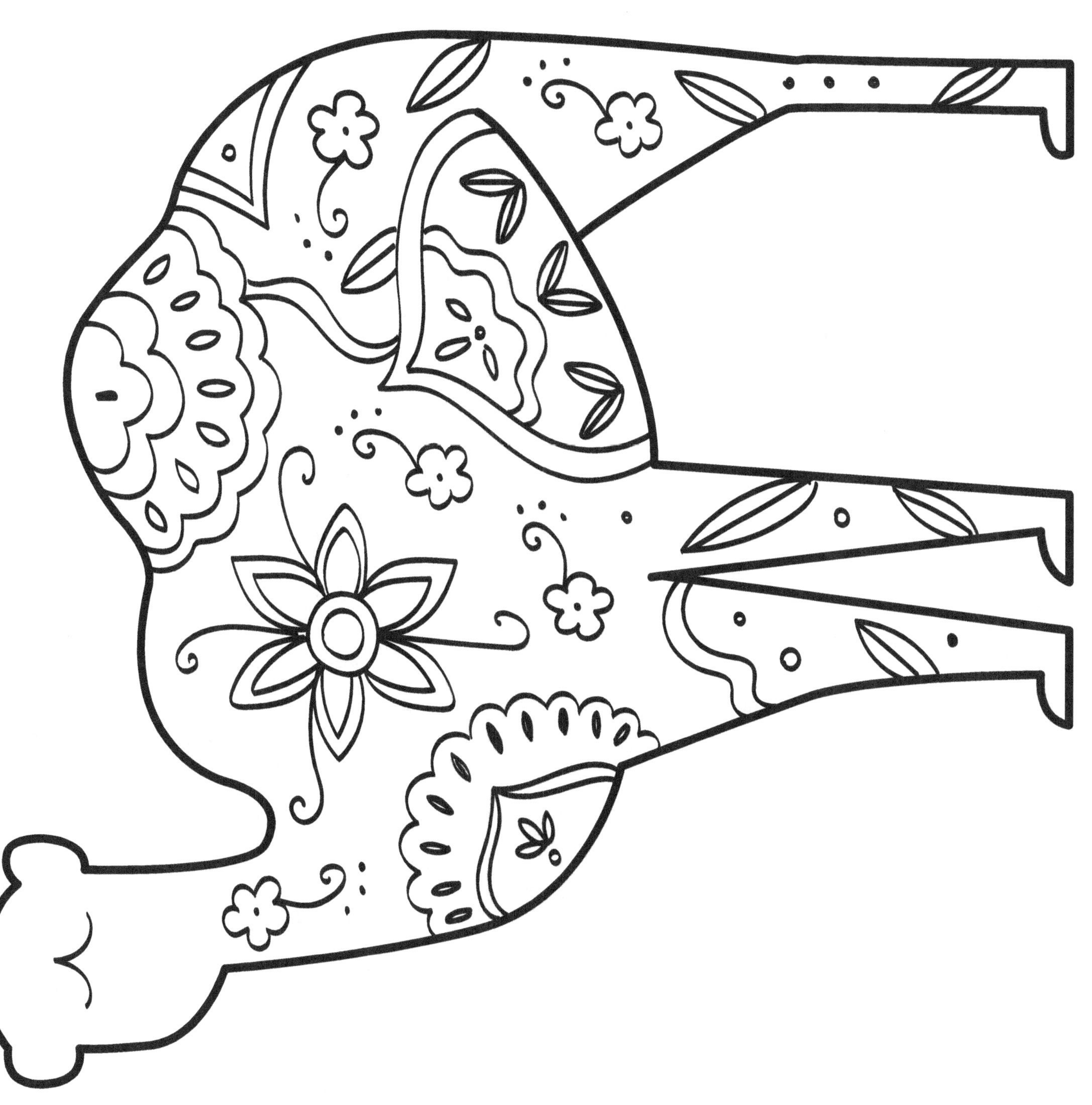

thank you,

..love you

thank you,

..love you

thank you,

..love you

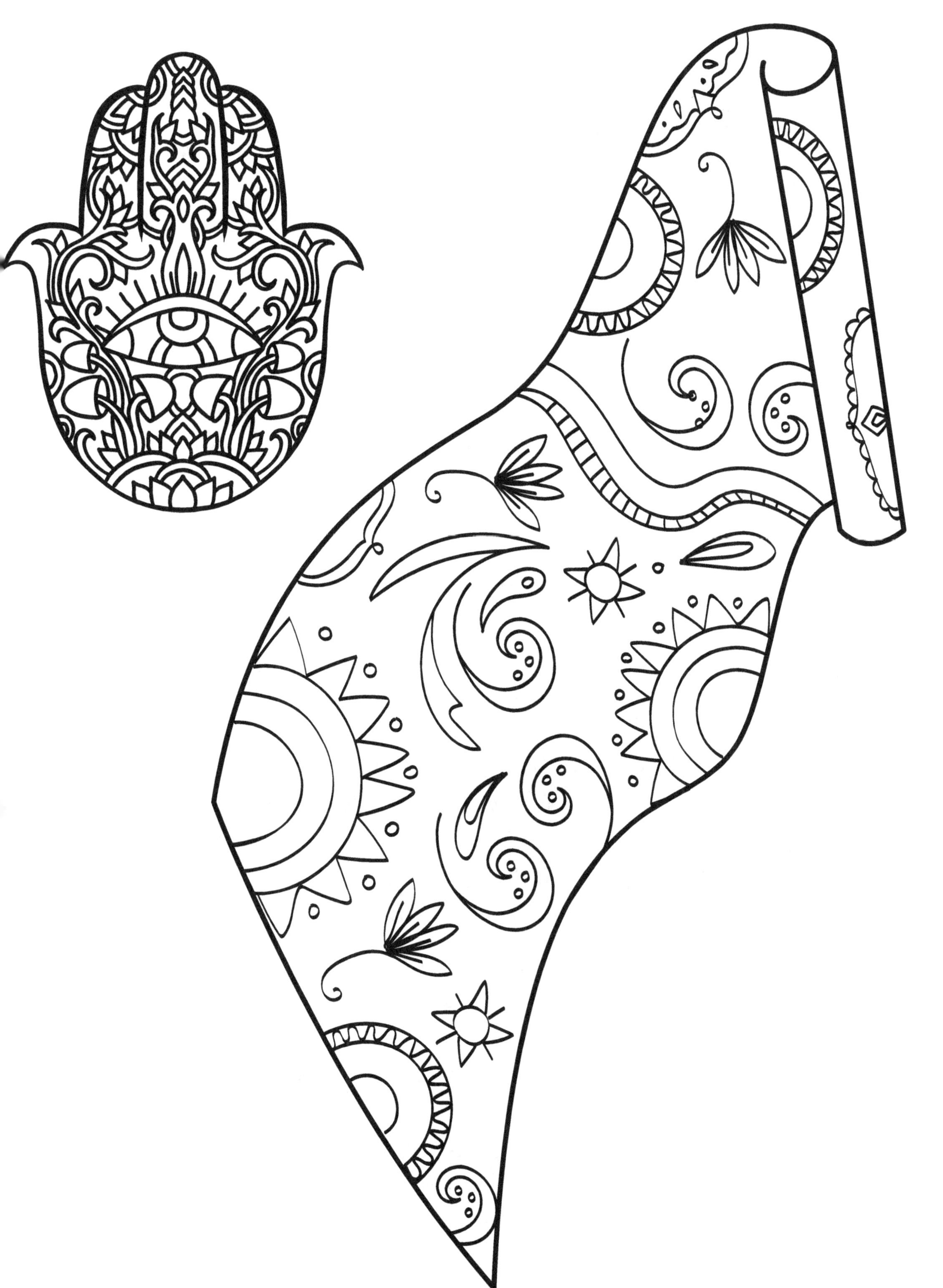

thank you,

..love you

thank you,

..love you

thank you,

..love you

thank you,

..love you

thank you,

..love you

thank you,

..love you

thank you,

..love you

thank you,

..love you

thank you,

..love you

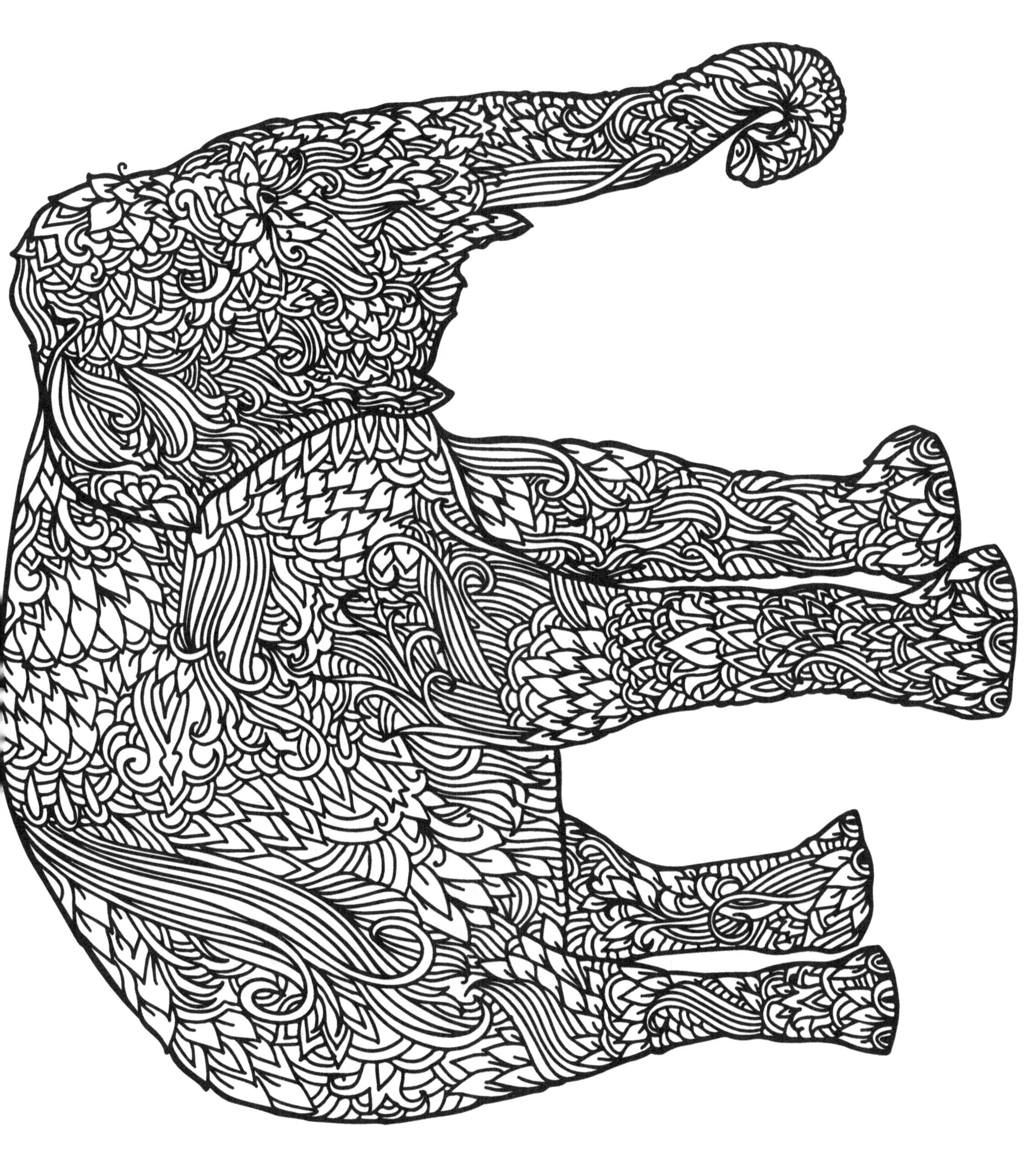

thank you,

..love you

thank you,

..love you

thank you,

..love you

thank you,

..love you